TRAIN FOR JOY

Break The Five Toxic Beliefs That Hold You Back From Success

By

CORINNA KONG

COPYRIGHT NOTICE

LEGAL DISCLAIMERS

The author and publisher shall not be liable for your misuse of this material. This book is strictly for informational and educational purposes.

The purpose of this book is to educate and entertain. The author or publisher do not guarantee that anyone following these techniques, suggestions, tips, ideas, or strategies will become successful. The author /or publisher shall have neither liability nor responsibility to anyone with respect to any loss or damage caused, or alleged to be.

This book is designed to provide information from a coaching perspective but not a counseling or therapy perspective. Coaching is different from counseling or therapy. Coaching starts with where you are and focuses on where you want to go. It's not about the past or what has transpired to this point. It's always focused on taking intentional actions.

To all who want to achieve success on your own terms—

Don't allow stress and anxiety to run your life

CONTENTS

FREE BONUSES For You:

Download 7 Minutes To Increase Your Happiness FREE Guide (Retail value: $15)

www.gohappyyou.com/p/happiness-hacks

Download 21 Thinking Habits For Success Self-Coaching FREE Workbook (Retail value: $35)

https://www.gohappyyou.com/p/21-thinking-habits-for-success

Get FREE Self-Doubt Detox Strategy Session (Retail value: $375)

https://www.gohappyyou.com/p/self-doubt-detox

Join Train For Joy Private Facebook Community

https://www.facebook.com/groups/256238091871338/?ref=group_header

COACHING PROGRAMS For Your Success And Happiness:

https://www.gohappyyou.com/p/programs

TrainForJoy™ -Learned Positively! Group Coaching

TransformU™—From Fears To Actions! Webinar Coaching

TheGoalGym™-Achieve Anything You Want! Individual Coaching

MobileU™—Combat The Daily Grind! Text-Based Coaching

INTRODUCTION

I am a Chinese who grew up in a once British colony—Hong Kong. In 1997, Hong Kong was returned to China, according to an agreement signed between China and Britain more than 120 years ago. Serendipity led me to the right place—I embarked on a new journey to San Francisco, California, United States in 1998. I did not plan to immigrate to America, but I have resided in San Francisco since then. Many oriental cultures believe in fate, but I believe in destiny.

Our beliefs are shaped by our upbringings and the expectations of our cultures. I have been caught among three different countries, customs, and cultures. Though I have been caught among three different sets of cultures, one societal value stands true across the cultures, that is— SUCCESS. You are expected to be successful in the eyes of others.

Becoming successful was the core pursuit of my life. When I was a child, I was expected to become successful in the eyes of my parents and society. Money, fame, and status—that's all we ought to pursue.

My father told me I was imaginative, curious, and hard-working. Among the three of my qualities, only one mattered to him—hard-working. Because then, I'd be able to achieve the success that he wanted me to have.

Now, when I look back at my younger self, I realize I have always been a dreamer. I dream dreams. I achieve dreams. I think life would be boring and meaningless if I stop dreaming.

When I was a young child, I dreamed of becoming a fashion designer, an opera singer, and an author. However, I didn't really achieve my dreams back then because my father said those dreams were impractical. He wanted me to become a lawyer. Though I didn't think I would ever become a fashion designer, opera singer, or an author, I did take professional classes to develop my skills in opera singing and fashion design. And I write at leisure.

When I was growing up, I never really bought into the practical dreams of success—money, fame, and status. Against the will of my father, I chose to become a social worker. I worked in a major hospital in Hong Kong, which functioned as emergency rooms for acute cases. I had seen dreams shattered and how lives were taken away by sicknesses, senseless tragedies, and unwise decisions. My father and mother passed away in the same hospital where I worked. Back then, I was just a young single woman in my 20s. I felt like an orphan after they passed. I sank into depression for two years. I know first-hand the pursuit of happiness is more than skin deep.

After my parents passed on, I wanted to start a new life somewhere else. Again, serendipity led me to the right place—I ran into an old friend, who invited me to advance my education in America. I said yes. That has changed my career trajectory and life since then. For the past 14 years, I have helped professionals and leaders in various technology companies and NGOs in Silicon Valley achieve their professional and personal excellence through training and coaching.

I believe in destiny. I believe everyone has destiny calls. And your destiny can be altered by the actions you take and the decisions you make. What actions are you going to take, and what decisions are you going to make to fulfill your destiny?

Today, I am energized, vibrant, and happy, but it wasn't always that way…there was a time in my life when I was unhappy, depressed, and stuck.

I grew up in a shame-based culture and a dysfunctional family. The toxic beliefs that I believed had kept me from reaching the success

I'd wanted. I thought I was not creative enough to become a fashion designer. I thought I was not talented enough to become an opera singer. I thought I would never be able to write a book. I thought my father was right—I was not good enough.

Toxic beliefs had limited my potentials and stopped me from pursuing my dreams. As I mentioned earlier, our deliberate actions and decisions would alter our destinies. When I embarked on a new journey in America, I decided to give myself permission to live my true self and achieve success on my own terms.

I allowed myself to study everything that'd interested me—from computer sciences to graphic design, from accounting to electronic music sequencing, from educational technology to digital marketing, from dancing to singing.

Do you know? You have unlimited potential, and you possess multiple intelligences. Educational psychologists have identified seven distinct bits of intelligence we possess—language, logical-mathematical analysis, spatial representation, musical thinking, the use of the body to solve problems. [1] What does it mean? You can achieve any dreams you want, and you can do anything you set your mind to. But you need to know what you really want.

What do you REALLY want in life and career?

Have toxic beliefs been limiting your potential?

Do you believe you have a destiny and you are capable of living it or losing it?

Where are you in life right now?

Are you a dreamer-in-heart?

Do you have big dreams?

Have you accomplished your big dreams yet?

Or have you forgotten your big dreams already?

Are you reluctant to step out of your comfort zone for fear of failure?

Are you still living under the shadow of your parents' dreams?

Are you feeling lonely, stressed, or depressed achieving the success you think you want?

Are you achieving the success that someone else wants for you?

What do you REALLY want?

Are you hoping for a breakthrough in your personal and professional life?

Again, what do you REALLY want?

Do you want to achieve your own dreams?

Do you want to achieve more and stress less?

Do you want to honor your needs and become happier?

Do you want to have better relationships at home and work?

Do you have bigger dreams?

What has been holding you back from achieving your dreams?

To all who want to achieve success on your own terms—

Don't allow stress and anxiety to run your life

Where are you in life?

You work hard. You are accomplished. You've paid the price. Your success has taken a toll on you. You don't know where you are heading anymore. You are disoriented. You think you are wasting your time and your life. You feel stuck and unhappy.

Somehow, you believe in a lie that you need to have it all—a great career, a successful business, a happy marriage, and beautiful smart kids. You know that's a lie. But you are afraid of admitting that you've believed in the lie because people around you expect you to keep going. They say, "You're doing so well. What's wrong?" But you say to yourself, "I think maybe there is something wrong with me."

The truth could be—your children are off-course. Or you are about to get a divorce. Or you are afraid of being demoted or laid-off. Or you are going to run out of business. Or you've gotten ill, but you couldn't tell anyone. Or you're losing your loved ones, but you have to act strong. No one could understand your pain. Life is messy.

You are overwhelmed, disoriented, and unhappy. You feel stuck, but you always look good on the outside. No one knows you feel very lonely inside. You always have a smile on your face. But deep down, you are filled with self-doubt, fear, and anxiety.

Or you are the superstar of your team. But deep down, you hate your job. You hate having to choose between work and family all the time. You persevere. But your light is almost out. You feel miserable.

You're not alone. You can be happy and successful by staying true to yourself and standing up for your own values. You need to say yes to yourself and live your priorities. Are you living your "real" priorities or someone else's priorities?

Saying yes to yourself means saying no to many things, AND, you will disappoint many people. But then, you will set yourself up for success and live a life of joy, purpose, and fulfillment. It's your choice.

Happiness is a choice. Happiness may not come knocking on your door, but you can increase your happiness through deliberate actions. Taking one small step at a time. Putting one foot in front of the other. You can build a meaningful life.

My mission is to help you fulfill your purpose, live your real priorities, create a new roadmap to achieve the success you want with more joy and less stress. But you ought to break the toxic beliefs that have stalled you so that you can unlock locked doors and get to a place of freedom, self-actualization, truth, and authentic happiness.

As I mentioned earlier, I grew up in a shame-based culture and a dysfunctional family. I became a people pleaser because that's the only way I knew to do. To survive, I had to constantly seek approvals from my father and the people around me—teachers, friends, and even strangers!

Eventually, I embarked on a journey of self-discovery and healing. And I have unlearned all these five toxic beliefs! Through years of struggling, learning, relearning, and persevering, I uncovered a few secrets of living a joyful life. Now, I would like to share with you the secrets.

LET ME ASK YOU ONE MORE TIME...WHAT DO YOU REALLY WANT?

What do you REALLY want to have accomplished in your life?

What would you like your loved ones to say about you at your funeral?

If you can achieve any dreams you want, what would you like to have achieved in the next five years, ten years, or twenty years? Why?

Are you ready for a change? Change is good.

You can take small actions to achieve big goals. You can achieve any dreams you set your mind to. Don't underestimate the power of your dreams. It is time to live your real priorities and achieve your dreams.

WHAT'S AHEAD?

This book presents a coaching, behavioral, and spiritual framework for examining the thoughts that contribute to your actions.

You can build stronger thinking habits by applying the actionable advice of this book. Then, you will begin to keep the toxic beliefs from limiting your life, lessening your self-confidence, and sabotaging your relationships.

This book is designed to provide information from a coaching perspective but not a counseling or therapy angle. Coaching is different from counseling or therapy. Coaching starts with where you are and focuses on where you want to go. It's not about the past. It's always focused on taking intentional actions to accomplish your goals.

Here is an overview of this book.

Chapter 1:

Think About Your Thoughts; You Are More Than Your Thoughts

Your subconscious mind drives your thoughts, feelings, and actions. And your actions will determine the long-term outcomes of your life. Therefore, think right. When you change your thoughts, you can change your life.

Chapter 2:

Toxic Belief #1: People-Pleasing

You Think, "I Can't Say No."

You are gentle, kind, and loving. People like you. So, people give you responsibilities that you don't ask for. People call you at inconvenient times. You accept any tasks that come your way, and you answer most of the calls. However, you have become exhausted, angry, and stressed. You think, "How come I just can't say no?" Because you feel guilty saying no.

Chapter 3:

Toxic Belief #2: Self-Doubting

You Think, "I Am Not Good Enough."

You are in charge of situations, people, and projects, but you never think you are good enough. You think everybody else is doing better than you do. You believe that you are inadequate and mediocre although evidence shows you are highly skilled and you are the expert. Paradoxically, you may even have a fear of success.

Chapter 4:

Toxic Belief #3: Perfectionism

You think, "I can't accept any standard short of perfection."

You set extremely high standard for yourself and/or others. You believe you need to be perfect, and you expect the people around you to be perfect. You are resentful when you or others do not meet your high standard. You become depressed when not meeting your goals. It's a painful journey living as a perfectionist.

Chapter 5:

Toxic Belief #4: Fear of Rejection

You Think, "I Need To Avoid Taking Risks That Can Result In Failures."

Rejection hurts. Because it makes you feel less than, not enough, and helpless. Rejection is different from failure; failure happens to your plans, but rejection happens to you. The good news is that you can unlearn helplessness and overcome the fear of rejection. You can create options for yourself. You can also gain self-acceptance through deliberate actions.

Chapter 6:

Toxic Belief #5: Self-Condemnation

You Think, "That's My Fault."

You have a negative inner critic, and you judge yourself all the time. You tell yourself, "I should have been more successful," "I should have done better," "I should have been a better spouse and parent," "I should have been perfect," "I should have landed that job or earned that promotion." You compare yourself with others and feel falling short.

Chapter 7: Closing Words

You Are Made For More; You Can Train Yourself For Joy

You are more than your thoughts. You can change your thoughts. You can unlearn helplessness and learn to be optimistic. You have more control over the outcomes of your life than you think. When you change your thoughts, you can change your life. Let's train for joy.

Dear readers,

Don't forget to claim your gifts!

Claim Your FREE BONUSES now.

Download 7 Minutes To Increase Your Happiness FREE Guide (Retail value: $15)

www.gohappyyou.com/p/happiness-hacks

Download 21 Thinking Habits For Success Self-Coaching FREE Workbook (Retail value: $35)

https://www.gohappyyou.com/p/21-thinking-habits-for-success

Get FREE Self-Doubt Detox Strategy Session (Retail value: $375)

https://www.gohappyyou.com/p/self-doubt-detox

Join Train For Joy Private Facebook Community

https://www.facebook.com/groups/256238091871338/?ref=group_header

Your Joy Coach & Success Strategist, Corinna Kong

www.gohappyyou.com

Connect with me on social media

Facebook: @trainforjoy @gohappyyou

Instagram: @corinna.kong

Pinterest: https://www.pinterest.com/corinnakong/

LinkedIn: https://www.linkedin.com/in/corinnakong

CHAPTER ONE

THINK ABOUT YOUR THOUGHTS

You Are More Than Your Thoughts

Dorothy was a budding entrepreneur. People thought she's confident, but deep down, she didn't believe in herself. Her mentors affirmed her that she had the capabilities and talent to build successful businesses. With their encouragements, she decided to step into entrepreneurship. She was intelligent and diligent. She had initial successes with a social enterprise. She asked for a coaching conversation to help her move past her fear of failures and self-doubt. Let's take a look at the coaching conversation with Dorothy.

Coach: Congratulations on your new endeavor of starting a new business.

Dorothy: I am scared. I am not sure if I can handle that.

Coach: I remember your mentors thought highly of you?

Dorothy: Yes, it's very kind of them, and I appreciate their encouragement. People think entrepreneurs are risk-takers. But I don't think I'm much of a risk-taker.

Coach: How so?

Dorothy: Well, I have to be honest with you, I feel scared most of the time when taking a risk. [Laughing nervously]

Coach: I understand your hesitation because it's never easy for anyone to take any risks. To me, you look confident and self-assured.

Dorothy: You've heard that, "fake it till you make it," right? [Laughing nervously]

Coach: So you think you need to fake it?

Dorothy: Well…yes

Coach: I can understand your feeling of apprehension. Would it be okay to explore how we can work together to help you expand your self-perception?

Dorothy: Yes, okay.

Coach: Would you share with me a big accomplishment that you've achieved for the past couple of years?

Dorothy: Years ago, I helped a social enterprise build a new program that benefited thousands of underserved kids. That made me happy. [There's a smile on her face]

Coach: It looks like you're most proud of your contribution to better the kids' lives.

Dorothy: Yes, the kids' smiles made my day!

Coach: Now, let's imagine…what would you like to have accomplished one year after building this business?

Dorothy: Hmm…[Her eyes closed] I imagine I am celebrating with the community of people I serve…just feel good.

Coach: It sounds like you really enjoy the community and the impact that you'll make to the people you serve.

Dorothy: Yes.

Coach: Now, examine your confidence level again. How confident are you now?

Dorothy: Wow…I feel way more confident now…because I know why I am building this business. Thank you!

Do you know? When you focus on fears, you stop your actions. When you focus on possibilities, you'll take positive actions to create the future you want.

CHANGE YOUR THOUGHTS. CHANGE YOUR LIFE

Research [1] shows that our thoughts and imaginations have the power to control our genes and our brains. [2] Thus, our thoughts have the power to create the life we want or ruin it.

You have heard, "You are what you think all day long." But the truth is that you are more than your thoughts! The frontal lobe of our brain allows us to stand outside of us to observe our thoughts according. We can observe our thoughts and decide what we choose to think about. Each moment is a new decision moment, and you can choose either positive or negative thoughts. Eventually, your thoughts are going to determine your course of actions and the outcomes of your life. Every moment, you have the power to change the course of your destiny in a good way or in a bad way. Now, what would you choose to think about?

At this moment, you are probably thinking about whether you should continue reading this book. You may think the information is insightful. Or you may also become skeptical about the information. Your thinking right now will determine whether you'd choose to continue reading. If you think you don't trust the information or you don't trust me, you would probably choose to close this book. If you think the information is interesting and useful, you will choose to continue reading. Do you know? You make over 35,000 decisions a day. All these decisions will shape your day, life, and destiny. Think wisely.

Now, let's reflect on your thoughts. What thoughts came across your mind the past hour? What thoughts have you been cultivating? Were they delightful or stressful thoughts? Now, let's sit still for five minutes and examine your thoughts. Notice your emotional and physical reactions. Is your palm tighten up? Do you feel a rush of blood flowing to your body? Are you embarrassed by the mistakes you made yesterday? Are you tearing up because of some painful memories that come up on your conscious mind? Watch your thoughts now. "Now" has presented a new opportunity for you to change your thoughts. What would you choose? Would you choose happy thoughts or stressful thoughts? Or have you determined to let your negative thoughts run their courses? This moment, you have the power to change the course of your life and your destiny. What would you choose? Would you choose to seize the moment and turn off your negative thoughts now?

I'm sure you've experienced this before. The painful memories of your past—the past hurts, failures, and rejections show up without invitations. Do you know? Scientific research shows that you can rewire your memories because your long-term memories aren't stable and they can change over time. And you can change the emotions associated with your memories. That means, **now is the moment to change your past.**

Whenever you recall your memories, there are emotions attached to the memories. Let's say, when you recall the memories of your recent breakup, you may tear up and experience the sorrows all over again. Every time you recall that painful memory, you are re-strengthening the connections between that memory and your emotions. However, science has made possible to edit bad memories and remove the bad feelings associated with those memories. [3]

How so?

Scientists mentioned that our memories can be modified with new information. [4]

The implications are—we not only can rewire our memories, but we can also reprogram the emotions associated with the memories. Instead of adding sorrows to your bitter memories, would you like to sweeten your memories now?

You have choices. You can choose your thoughts. You are more than your thoughts. Your thoughts can change your brain, thus, change your life.

YOUR BELIEFS WILL DETERMINE THE OUTCOMES OF YOUR LIFE

What is a belief? A belief defines an idea or principle which we judge to be true. Then, how would our beliefs determine the outcomes of our lives?

Do you have friends, co-workers, or relatives who are habitually negative? They believe their circumstances are unchangeable, that means, they believe nothing they could do to change their circumstances? They end up doing nothing about it and choosing to be miserable. Do you have this kind of friends or relatives? I bet you do. When they habitually think their life is miserable, they then become helpless. They choose not to confront the realities, and they stay stuck.

On the contrary, do you know people who always have a positive outlook on life and they believe in a brighter future, even if they are actually "in a pit"? Their life circumstances may be difficult, but they never give up fighting for a better future. They end up creating the success they've wanted.

Let's get inside the minds of these two types of people— optimists and pessimists. For those, people who believe the courses of setbacks in their lives are temporary and changeable, do not become helpless. We call them optimist. Conversely, people who habitually think their setback is going to last forever and undermine everything, and that there is nothing they can do about it, we call them pessimists. [5] Examine your habitual thought patterns. Because your habitual thoughts will either enable you to build a joyful and successful life or a miserable one. Which life would you like to choose? If your thought patterns are mostly negative, you will have to pay close attention to how they impact your life and relationships. Research found that pessimists are more ready to get depressed and underachieved.

At this moment, you may have a hard time figuring out whether you are an optimist or a pessimist. To find out, you can reflect on your "habitual" thought patterns. Or you can ask your significant others to help you. We all become negative about life and circumstances *at times*. But it does not make you a pessimist. What you need to examine are your *habitual thought patterns* and your beliefs.

Let me ask you a few more questions to clarify your thoughts. Do you have a good sense of personal control (i.e., the ability to change things by voluntary actions)? Do you feel helpless easily? Do you have a pessimistic or optimistic outlook on life?

The good news is—whether you are a pessimist or an optimist, you can learn to become an optimist through developing new sets of cognitive skills. It's called learned optimism. [5] You can learn to talk yourself through personal defeat. You can reappraise and reframe your setbacks, and you can turn to believe your setbacks are just temporary. You can compartmentalize your failure in certain areas of your life. You can tell yourself—though you fail in certain areas of your life, you are not a failure. At this moment, it is important to shake off the label of success that our society has imposed on you.

You can choose to think about what you can learn from your past failures and mistakes. You can choose to do things differently next time. I assure you, when you choose to learn optimism, you will live a better life with more self-acceptance.

EXERCISE: HOW TO BREAK NEGATIVE SELF-TALK

To increase self-acceptance, we must break our negative self-talk. You can follow the instructions as shown below to start breaking your negative self-talk on a daily basis.

1. Create two columns on your journal

2. Write down your negative self-talk on the left-hand column

3. Write down evidence to defend yourself on the right-hand column

4. Cross out your negative self-talk one by one

5. Write a set of new beliefs to replace the negative ones

6. Read it aloud to yourself at least once a day

CONCLUSION

Remember, you are more than your thoughts. Your thoughts have the power to propel you forward or to keep you from reaching your goals and realizing your greatest potential. You have the power to change your habitual thought patterns and reprogram your brain. You can choose thoughts that empower you. Because your thoughts can turn certain genes on and certain genes off [1]. Your thoughts can change your brain, thus change the outcomes of your life. You have a bright future ahead of you. You can achieve big dreams and goals. Believe it now!

You are made for more. Train yourself for joy. And you will then be able to change the outcomes of your life. This is what this book is about.

FREE BONUSES:

Download 7 Minutes To Increase Your Happiness FREE Guide (Retail value: $15)

www.gohappyyou.com/p/happiness-hacks

Download 21 Thinking Habits For Success Self-Coaching FREE Workbook (Retail value: $35)

https://www.gohappyyou.com/p/21-thinking-habits-for-success

Get FREE Self-Doubt Detox Strategy Session (Retail value: $375)

https://www.gohappyyou.com/p/self-doubt-detox

Join Train For Joy Private Facebook Community

https://www.facebook.com/groups/256238091871338/?ref=group_header

CHAPTER TWO

PEOPLE-PLEASING

You Think, "I Can't Say No."

"After living with their dysfunctional behavior for so many years, people become invested in defending their dysfunctions rather than changing them." ~Marshall Goldsmith

Katherine was a highly respected manager. Her management thought she did a fantastic job to delight the customers. But what they didn't know—she consistently worked over 12 hours a day to keep up with her work, and she's on the verge of burnout. Because of her capability of getting things done, her management gave her more and more responsibilities. She was overworked, but she had a hard time saying no to new responsibilities. She failed to ask for help either because she's afraid that it would make her look incompetent.

Her workload had prohibited her from spending time with her family. She felt isolated. She had fierce arguments with her husband because of her priorities. She neglected her self-care. She started experiencing symptoms of back pain and panic attacks. She couldn't sleep well at night and at times, had nightmares. In many of her nightmares, she saw herself being fired from her job and getting a divorce.

Her parents also demanded a lot from her. For this reason, her husband had grown even more resentful of her. She didn't feel supported and loved. But she chose to compromise because she's a people pleaser.

Her life looked perfect on the outside, but she was miserable on the inside. People thought she had it all. But deep down, she felt resentful, bitter, and depressed. She was overwhelmed. She felt like a pushover. Yet, she continued to say yes to responsibilities that she didn't want to take.

People pleasers needed approvals from others. In exchange for approvals, Katherine sacrificed her happiness, health, and well-being. She's a people pleaser, and she's miserable.

ARE YOU A PEOPLE PLEASER?

Let's take a self-assessment. How strongly do you agree with the following statements?

*1. Strongly Disagree; 2. Disagree; 3. Neutral; 4. Agree; 5. Strongly Agree

- I am not honest with others about my feelings and thinking

- I avoid conflicts and confrontations

- I do things out of duty or obligations

- I constantly sacrifice my own legitimate needs

- I have a strong desire to be liked and accepted

- I am keen on seeking approvals from others

- I apologize a lot

- I tend not to say no to external requests and demands?

- I feel guilty saying no

When you agree or strongly agree with most of the above statements, you are a people pleaser.

THE ROOT CAUSE OF PEOPLE-PLEASING

A people pleaser is afraid of losing love. A people pleaser wants to be needed. The root cause of people-pleasing—people pleasers do not feel worthy.

In order to feel worthy, a people pleaser seeks constant approvals from others. A people pleaser can't say no because she/he is so afraid of being rejected and abandoned. Again, a people pleaser desperately needs love.

Also, a people pleaser don't know how to say no because a people pleaser feels guilty when saying no. A people pleaser thinks she/he is a bad person when saying no. A people pleaser cannot embrace her/his inadequacies or badness.

When we cannot embrace our badness, we would pretend to be better than we actually are—people-pleasing behaviors temporarily makes us feel worthy, accepted, and loved. A people pleaser wants to be needed, so she/he just won't say no. A people pleaser does not want to shun love and needs approvals from others.

WHAT'S THE PROBLEM OF PEOPLE-PLEASING?

Being a people pleaser, very likely, you have critical parents. Your parents may not be satisfied with who you truly are. They covertly or overtly want you to be someone they want you to be. As a grown-up, you still have the need to satisfy your parents' demands. You say yes to their demands and say no to your legitimate needs.

What are the problems of being a people pleaser? You are overloaded with responsibilities. You are constantly stressed and unhappy. You sacrifice your well-being in exchange for acceptance of others. In the long run, people-pleasing behaviors will negatively impact your physical and emotional health. And your love tank will deplete.

I used to be a people pleaser. My father couldn't accept who I was (I thought he wished me to be a boy). He criticized me as too curious, too vain, and too bad. Therefore, I thought I was a bad person, a really bad person. I thought, "If I were a good person, my father would have accepted me." I felt no self-worth being a girl when growing up. So, I studied extra hard to "prove" that I was worthy. I also had an intense need to please others, including strangers. Crazy, isn't it?

People-pleasing drove me to depression. I remembered when I was under ten years old; my friends told me I was an unhappy person. I rarely had a smile on my face. Then I started to please them by pretending to be happier than I was. I was miserable. Interestingly, people pleasers are surrounded by critical people. People pleasers are incongruent and deeply unhappy. I believe many people pleasers also live with high-functioning depression.

Today, I am no longer a people pleaser.

So, you may ask, "How do you break your people-pleasing behaviors?"

I sought professional help. I also learned many secrets to keep people-pleasing from impacting my life negatively.

I would like to share with you my secrets.

The #1 secret of breaking people-pleasing beliefs, that is, change the way you see yourself!

First of all, you need to recognize that you own your thoughts, decisions, and the consequences of your behaviors. Your parents and other people don't own you. YOU ARE WORTHY. You don't need others to approve that you are worthy.

Secondly, you need to recognize that there are negative consequences of being a people pleaser. When you continue to please others, your love tank will be depleted. And you will then be deprived of love. And more importantly, you will not be able to live a purposeful, authentic, and joyful life. Do you want to live a joyless life? I bet I know your answer.

Bronnie Ware, the author of *The Top Five Regrets of the Dying* [1], opines that people regretted not living a more authentic life and being true to themselves.

Do you want to live a life of meaning and joy?

Do you want to honor your needs and wants?

Do you want to be true to yourself?

If so, you need to change the way you see yourself.

So, what's holding you back from living a joyful life and reaching your potential?

Here, I'd like to share some practical steps to help you break your people-pleasing beliefs.

HOW TO BREAK PEOPLE-PLEASING BELIEFS

1. Recognize you have legitimate needs

You need to recognize you have legitimate needs. More importantly, it is necessary to satisfy your legitimate needs. And it is not selfish to love yourself. Because then, you'll know how to love the people around you. Say no to excessive demands from others. Set some healthy boundaries with others. You have choices. You can choose to live a life of joy and meaning. You can choose to believe you are worthy. You are good enough. Do it today. Say no to responsibilities and treatments that you do not want.

2. Honor not only your needs but also your wants

You need to honor both your needs and wants. When you are thirsty, you need to drink. When you are hungry, you need to eat. When you are tired, you need to rest. You have dreams and desires. You are free to create a life that you want to live. Claim your freedom now and free yourself from condemnations, judgments, and guilt. When you dare to say no to excessive demands that you do not want to honor, in turn, other people will honor you.

3. Say no with tact and grace

First of all, you need to "want to change." Then, you'll need to "get ready" to change. Very importantly, you'll need an accountability partner to hold you responsible for making positive changes. That's a big step forward. You'll be apprehensive. You'll be tempted to give up. There are some practical steps. You can start by writing down the responsibilities that you don't want to take or keep. Then, you can write scripts for the conversations that you need to have with others. Don't skip the step of getting feedback from your accountability partner. Then, you'll need to practice delivering the message with tact and grace.

4. Practice self-love

Over the years of working with accomplished professionals, I've noticed that many of you do not know your "real" priorities. That's one of the reasons you don't honor your priorities. Not surprisingly, very few people know to prioritize self-love. Love yourself. I say it again, love yourself. I challenge you—this weekend, reflect on what it means to love yourself. It could be scheduling quiet time with yourself on a regular basis. It could be asking your spouse to help you with chores so you can have a night out with friends. It could be taking your kids to a nanny so that you can have alone time with your spouse. It could be making arrangements with your management to adjust your workload. It could be asking for new headcount to lighten your load. Remember, you need to honor your needs, protect your priorities, and say no to responsibilities that you don't want. Finally, you'll then be able to make room for your dreams. Live a good life. Live a purposeful life. You know you have choices. Prioritize self-love. Live your real priorities.

5. You can pray

I'd like to share with you some scientific data about prayers. Neuroscientists proved that prayer elicits feelings of love and compassion, there is a release of serotonin and dopamine. Serotonin has a direct impact on your mood, and not having enough serotonin has been linked to depression. Dopamine, on the other hand, is associated with reward and motivation.[2] Maybe you can pray.

6. Get ready to receive love

Not everyone is ready to receive love. Some people shun love because of low self-esteem. They think they are not worthy to receive love. But it's not you. You can choose to receive love. You can also choose to love others. Pause for a few moments now: Taste and see the love in your life, which is as fresh as dew. Taste and see that your life is good. Be ready. Be blessed.

I WOULD LIKE TO AFFIRM YOU:

- You are good

- You are worthy

- You are loved

- You have unique talents, gifts, and strengths

- You will make good use of your talents, gifts, and strengths

- Your life is full of potential

- You will fulfill your potential

- You can say no

- You don't need to feel guilty saying no anymore

- You can say yes to happiness

- You can train yourself for joy

ACTIONABLE ADVICE:

- **Increase the awareness of your people-pleasing behaviors.** Start journaling. Keep a log. Count how many times you meant to say no but you turn out saying yes. Why? What are the negative consequences of saying yes? What are the benefits of saying no? Then, you can write down your feelings, thinking, and the results of your choices.

- **Get an accountability partner.** Who would enable you to say no more bravely? Who would hold you accountable for living a better life?

- **Uncover thought patterns that have kept you from honoring your legitimate needs.** Write down your negative self-talks, justifications, and self-denying thoughts. Then, you can choose to share with your accountability partner or someone you trust. You will then see your blind spots and design corrective actions that will lead to more happiness and fulfillment.

Stop pleasing others and start honoring your needs and wants. Live a happy and strong life. Cheers.

Claim Your FREE BONUSES:

Download 7 Minutes To Increase Your Happiness FREE Guide (Retail value: $15)

www.gohappyyou.com/p/happiness-hacks

Download 21 Thinking Habits For Success Self-Coaching FREE Workbook (Retail value: $35)

https://www.gohappyyou.com/p/21-thinking-habits-for-success

Get FREE Self-Doubt Detox Strategy Session (Retail value: $375)

https://www.gohappyyou.com/p/self-doubt-detox

Join Train For Joy Private Facebook Community

https://www.facebook.com/groups/256238091871338/?ref=group_header

CHAPTER THREE

SELF-DOUBTING

You Think, "I Am Not Good Enough."

"If you hear a voice within you say you cannot paint, then by all means paint and that voice will be silenced." – Vincent van Gogh

Dawn was an ambitious and accomplished career woman. Since she was a child, her father told her that she ought to climb up the corporate ladder. It turned out, climbing the corporate ladder had become a unique way that she honored her father. Not only that, achieving career success had made her feel worthy of respect. Success had given her a sense of self-worth.

She had to win out her male counterparts at work. She asked for a major promotion, but she was told to "wait." She was very frustrated and unhappy. Her self-doubt prohibited her from experiencing the joy in life. She began to have symptoms of depression, insomnia, and migraine.

She doubted whether she would ever get the promotion. But she was reluctant to leave for a new work environment where she had to prove herself again. What made her even more unsettled—she was worried that one of her peers would get the promotion! Her inner critic went like this: "If you're worthy and good enough, you would have gotten that promotion."

The scary feeling of shame and humiliation had paralyzed her. She told herself that she could not fail. She had an intense fear of failure and rejection. She's stressed and miserable. She thought, "Maybe I don't deserve good things in my life. Maybe I won't get what I've wanted. Maybe there's something wrong with me. Maybe I'm not good enough."

She was stuck, stressed, and unfulfilled. She was miserable.

I resonate with Dawn's fear of disappointing her father. I am an Asian. For Asians who have grown up in a shame-based culture, it's the most difficult thing to admit to ourselves, our families, and other loved ones that we have a problem and need help because it goes against cultural norms. [1]

Shame-based beliefs can also be formed when an individual was growing up in a dysfunctional family. In shame-based family norms, you would feel shameful when you are not able to meet your parents' high expectations for you. You think failure is not an option. People who have shame-based beliefs also have self-doubt.

Self-doubt causes anxiety. You compare yourself to others. You are anxious about losing the respect of others. You doubt your self-worth. You have a fear of *becoming* a failure. You avoid taking risks to achieve your dreams because you don't want to fail. Your inner critic says, "Don't step out of your comfort zone. What if you fail? You don't want to be a failure, do you?" The results are missed opportunities. You don't get to achieve your dreams and live a joyful life.

THE ROOT OF SELF-DOUBT

Do you know? Self-doubt is a *learned behavior*. You learned self-doubt through your family norms. Have you learned self-doubt? Let's take a self-assessment:

- Have you been avoiding change for fear of losing control?

- Have you been reluctant to take risks to achieve personal goals?

- Have you been discouraged from pursuing your passions and dreams?

- Have you been discouraged to make your own decisions?

- Have you been shamed for making wrong decisions?

- Have you doubted your judgments?

If your answer yes to most of the above questions, you have learned self-doubt. You feel not good enough. The good news—since self-doubt is a learned behavior, you can unlearn self-doubt!

Do you want to unlearn self-doubt?

You may ask, "How may I unlearn self-doubt?"

Neuroscience research suggests you can rewire your brain by thinking right. Because your brain is like plastic and it can change. It's called neuroplasticity. Neuroplasticity refers to your brain's ability to reorganize itself, both physically and functionally, throughout your life responding to your environment, behavior, thinking, and emotions.

Research shows our mind can change our brain, but not the other way around. The evidence is that—Neuroplasticity enables people to recover from stroke, injury, and birth abnormalities, overcome autism, ADD and ADHD, learning disabilities and other brain deficits, pull out of depression and addictions, and reverse obsessive-compulsive patterns. [2]

What do I want to say? Your mind has the power to change your life! You can choose to think right thoughts. You can decide to practice optimism. You can choose to unlearn self-doubt. You can choose to learn self-assurance. You can achieve your dreams. You can train yourself for joy, and you can achieve the success on your terms.

THE PROBLEM OF SELF-DOUBT

Self-doubt is problematic. When you choose to believe that you're not good enough, you'll not be able to reach your highest potential. You have the treasures in you, but you choose to hide them under the dirt of your self-doubt. You are talented, resourceful, and valuable. It's a waste of your life when you're not achieving your dreams. Stop putting a boulder in front of you and start going forward. Stop sabotaging yourself and start getting unstuck. Stop listening to your inner critic and start taking control of your life. Stop spinning your wheels. Crush self-doubt!

Another problem of self-doubt—it may potentially lead to serious ailments such as anxiety, depression, weight gain, high blood pressure, chronic fatigue, and heart disease. [3]

Commit to choose right thoughts.

Love your life and protect your health.

Crush self-doubt.

You may ask, "How would I crush self-doubt?"

The answer is—your mind can change your brain. You can do anything you set your mind to.

YOUR MIND CAN CHANGE YOUR BRAIN

Your mind can change your brain. You can build stronger thinking habits through deliberate practices. I am a brain-based coach trained by the NeuroLeadership Results Coaching Systems. I would like to share a few facts about the brain, habits, and memories:

1. **In the process of building new habits, you're weakening your old habits.** Each time your brain strengthens a connection to advance your mastery of a new skill, it also weakens other connections of neurons that weren't used at that precise moment. In other words, in the process of building a new habit, you also are weakening your old habits. [4] Let's say you want to

be braver. You can choose thoughts and actions that'll enable you to be brave and self-assured. Let's do this. Now pause. Recall some of your accomplishments in the past. What do you remember? How does it make you feel when you savor your accomplishments? I am sure now your self-doubt holds no truth. Do you know? Actions crush self-doubt. Do you know? You can take small actions to achieve big goals. Take one small action at a time. Put one foot in front of another. Don't stop taking actions. You will build new habits and achieve your success.

2. **It takes time and deliberation to sustain positive behavioral changes.** Positive behavioral changes will only become permanent when you practice your new thinking habits deliberately, over time. Don't be discouraged when you fail to crush self-doubt at the moment. We are all perfectly imperfect. Choose right thoughts. Don't stop practicing your new thinking habits.

3. **Your initial change has to be small and incremental.** Contrary to conventional wisdom, your initial change is not supposed to be big, but it is supposed to be small and incremental. Why? Because the anticipation of a big change will "activate fear" in the limbic system of your brain. When fear is activated, you'll procrastinate and stop making progress. You may want to quit. DO this— develop some morning rituals to create a happy mood. You can figure out what works for you—it could be meditation, listening to music, humming a song when driving, taking a shower, or jogging—whatever it is. Choose to do things that make you feel happy. Why? Neuroscience research shows that when you are slightly happy, you're more likely to generate creative insights and make good decisions.

4. **You can rewire your brain and change your memories.** Neuroscience research shows your brain rewires your memories every time you remember something in the past. Therefore, it is possible for you to intentionally edit bad memories to remove the bad feelings associated with those memories. [5] You are more than your thoughts. You can change and rewire your bad memories of past shame, guilt, and judgments. You can live a joyful life and create a better future for yourself.

5. **Visualization will forge a path for you to go forward.** When you doubt yourself, you're not likely to want to go forward and reach your goals. You will procrastinate. How could you stop procrastinating? Visualization is a powerful exercise that helps you create the preferred future in your mind, vividly. Visualization is a powerful tool to retrain your subconscious mind because it allows you to feel and experience a situation which hasn't happened yet, as if it were real. [6] Crush self-doubt. Visualize success.

I WOULD LIKE TO AFFIRM YOU:

- You are good enough

- You are worthy

- You have unique talents, gifts, and strengths

- You will make good use of your talents, gifts, and strengths

- Your life is full of opportunities

- You will reach your potential

- You can be happy AND successful

ACTIONABLE ADVICE:

- **Increase your awareness**: Write down your thoughts of self-doubt. Create two columns—column A contains your thoughts of self-doubt. Column B contains new empowering thoughts. For example, a self-doubt comment could be, "I am not good enough." An empowering comment could be a comment from your spouse, "You always make things look easy."

- Recall positive feedback you received from your significant others, managers, colleagues, customers, and business partners. Write them down in your journal. Pause. Relive the joy at the moment.

- Write down at least three things you appreciate about yourself. Be specific.

- Celebrate your presence and your accomplishments.

- This week, **DO** one thing that causes you to step out of your comfort zone.

- **Receive self-love**: Write a love letter to yourself. Open your heart to allow love in.

Claim Your FREE BONUSES:

Download 7 Minutes To Increase Your Happiness FREE Guide (Retail value: $15)

www.gohappyyou.com/p/happiness-hacks

Download 21 Thinking Habits For Success Self-Coaching FREE Workbook (Retail value: $35)

https://www.gohappyyou.com/p/21-thinking-habits-for-success

Get FREE Self-Doubt Detox Strategy Session (Retail value: $375)

https://www.gohappyyou.com/p/self-doubt-detox

Join Train For Joy Private Facebook Community

https://www.facebook.com/groups/256238091871338/?ref=group_header

CHAPTER FOUR

PERFECTIONISM

You Think, **"I can't accept any standard short of perfection."**

"Striving to better, oft we mar what's well" ~Shakespeare

Beth's parents were very demanding about her academic achievements. Eventually, Beth graduated from a prestige university and had a successful career.

Beth was talented, ambitious, and beautiful. However, she was extremely intolerant of imperfections. She was highly critical of the people around her. She could not tolerate the imperfections and mistakes of others.

On the other hand, she was very sensitive and defensive about other people's criticisms of her. She refused to listen to corrective feedback. Though she was able to win her customers over and excelled in the technical aspects of her job, she was criticized for not having effective leadership capabilities. She had not been promoted for some years. She resented not being promoted. She was dissatisfied at work.

She was not satisfied with her family life either. Deep down, she had hoped her husband to be smarter, more successful, and good enough for her. She had unrealistically high expectations for her daughter as well. She was deeply resentful of herself and her life.

She expected herself and her life to be perfect. She could not accept any standard short of perfection. She was beautiful, charming, and successful on the outside. However, she felt flawed, not good enough, and broken on the inside.

Out of deep self-hatred, she attempted suicide twice.

THE FACES OF PERFECTIONISM

Perfectionism is dangerous. Perfectionism is also a joy killer. It damages your relationships and steals your joy. Perfectionism is a sister of self-doubt. Psychological studies show that there are two types of perfectionists—outwardly and inwardly focused perfectionists.

You may focus inwardly. You feel not good enough, so you demand yourself to achieve more. You can barely handle failures because that would expose your imperfections. When it comes to completing work or projects, you tend to procrastinate because you want your project to be perfect and accepted with 100% approvals. When things do not happen as planned, you get depressed. You think you "should have" done better. You may miss project deadlines because you want the project delivery to be 120% perfect. You keep revising, improving, and perfecting the delivery because you need praise and approvals from others, especially the people you respect. You don't handle criticism well. When you anticipate criticisms on the horizon, you shrink back and procrastinate, so that you can avoid criticism. You may even have a fear of success—because you know when you become more successful, you may face more criticisms. You sabotage your success.

You may also focus outwardly. You want everyone around you to be perfect. You want everyone to meet your superior high standard. So, you seek to change your spouse, colleagues, friends, and children. You're always disappointed with people. Your demand for perfection drives people away. As a result, you feel lonely, depressive, and isolated.

Beth was an outwardly focused perfectionist. She was often frustrated with people, their performance, and behaviors. She set extremely high standard for others. She couldn't tolerate other people's mistake. However, she couldn't handle and accept criticisms. She thought she's perfect but other people weren't. Her high expectations and negative attitude toward others caused problems in her interpersonal relationships.

Having grown up in a shame-based culture and a dysfunctional family, I was an inwardly focused perfectionist (thankfully, I am no longer one). Being an inward perfectionist was painful. I sought approvals from others. I believed there was a right and wrong way to do things. I had to do it the right way. I was hard on myself, and I could not tolerate my errors. I constantly worried about how other people thought about me and my performance. When I made mistakes, I would be depressed for a few days because I felt shameful. I couldn't forgive myself because I thought I was not good enough. I endured great pain and suffered from depression. My inner critics kept telling me that I was a failure and I was a shame. Sounds horrible, isn't it?

At the root of perfectionism is usually an early experience of harsh parental guidance, blame, or punishment. The harsh corrections and judgments thus resulted in damaged self-esteem and self-worth of the perfectionists.

Perfectionism is directly connected to self-esteem—without a sense of security, a person may feel that it is necessary to do things perfectly. [1]

Perfectionism could result in major depression. [2] Psychologists mentioned that perfectionists who have a family history of depression might, therefore, be more biologically vulnerable to developing the psychological and physical symptoms of major depression, may be particularly sensitive to events that stimulate their self-doubt and fear of rejection or humiliation.

I broke free from perfectionism and depression years ago. After I broke free from perfectionism, I reminded myself every single day— progress is better than perfection. I want joy over perfection. I tell myself, "Just do it, and there is no right or wrong way to do things. You can be creative." When you are joyful, you will perform better and have better relationships. Think big picture. Make a decision today. Crush perfectionism.

HOW TO BREAK PERFECTIONISM

The suggestions here are based on my own experience. It's not supposed to be taken as psychotherapy advice. If you need psychotherapy advice, I suggest you seek counsel from a licensed therapist.

To break perfectionism, you need to be aware of your personality traits of perfectionism, and you need to recognize how it negatively impacted your well-being, relationships, and work performance. Then, you need to seek help and gain support from others. You cannot break perfectionism by your willpower. You won't succeed. Perfectionism is hard to break because our society somewhat celebrates the traits of perfectionism. To break perfectionism, you need a support system—support and encouragements from positive and like-minded people. AND, you will want to change. Because change is difficult. You may have to give up something less valuable in exchange for something more valuable. Failures and backslides are expected. That's why you need a good support system. Let's assess where you are and where you want to be.

1. **Are you aware of your personality traits of perfectionism?**

Do you agree with the following statements?

*1. Strongly disagree; 2. Disagree; 3. Neutral; 4. Agree; 5. Strongly agree

- Do you set unrealistically high standard for yourself?

- Do you set unrealistically high standard for others?

- Do you feel depressed when not meeting your own standard?

- Are you critical of yourself most of the times?

- Are you critical of others most of the times?

- Are you defensive of criticisms?

- Do you have a fear of failure?

- Do you have a fear of rejection?

- Do you procrastinate on taking actions?

- Do you avoid making mistakes?

- Do you feel bad about yourself when you make mistakes?

- Do you feel not good enough, even if you have accomplished a lot in life?

If you agree with most of these statements, you are very likely having a personality trait of perfectionism. If so, your well-being could have already been negatively impacted.

2. Do you want a positive change?

Do you want to make a positive change and live a better life? Reflect on the following thinking questions:

- Have your important relationships been negatively impacted due to your perfectionism? In what ways?

- Have you been struggling with negative emotions lately?

- What has been holding you back from making a positive change? Fear of uncertainty? Fear of stigma? Fear of losing respect? Low self-esteem? What else?

- Who and what will be at stake when you change?

- Who'd benefit from your change?

- How would your life be better when you make a positive change?

- How willing are you to change?

3. **Are you willing to get help?**

Take a long hard look at your relational life right now. Answer the following questions:

- Do you want to live a joyful life?

- What do you need to do in order to live a joyful life?

- How much do you want to get help?

- Name 3-5 people who care about your well-being and want the best for you.

- Write down practical ways that they could help you with.

- When are you going to reach out to them?

Again, are you willing to get help? The choices are yours. You are your decision maker.

ACTIONABLE ADVICE:

Here is some actionable advice to help you increase your self-awareness. Practice self-awareness often. Practicing mindfulness will also help boost your happiness over time.

- Meditate. Take deep breaths. Quiet your mind and bring your active thoughts into awareness. Notice your thoughts. Don't judge or condemn yourself.

- Write down your thoughts on your journal

- Notice your reactions when reading your thoughts. Feeling stressed? Sad?

- Read your thoughts from a "stranger's perspective." Imagine when you hear a stranger share with you the thoughts, what would you say to the stranger?

- Be compassionate to yourself. For inward perfectionists, you can create a new column in your journal—write down affirmations that you would like to hear. For example—"It's okay not being perfect," "you are a good person," "no one is perfect," "it's okay to make mistakes, you win some, and you learn some."

- Be compassionate to others. For outward perfectionists, create a new column in your journal—write down your assumptions about others' behaviors. Reflect on your expectations on others. You'll then adjust your standard.

Claim Your FREE BONUSES:

Download 7 Minutes To Increase Your Happiness FREE Guide (Retail value: $15)

www.gohappyyou.com/p/happiness-hacks

Download 21 Thinking Habits For Success Self-Coaching FREE Workbook (Retail value: $35)

https://www.gohappyyou.com/p/21-thinking-habits-for-success

Get FREE Self-Doubt Detox Strategy Session (Retail value: $375)

https://www.gohappyyou.com/p/self-doubt-detox

Join Train For Joy Private Facebook Community

https://www.facebook.com/groups/256238091871338/?ref=
group_header

CHAPTER FIVE

FEAR OF REJECTION

You Think, **"I Need To Avoid Taking Risks That Can Result In Failures."**

Lucia was a rising star in the company that she'd worked for over 15 years. One morning, her manager called her into his office. He delivered the bad news, "Lucia, I am sorry to tell you… I'll not be able to give you the promotion that I promised you a few months ago…because you are chosen to be a part of a layoff. It has nothing to do with your performance. I am reluctant to do that, but we have to lay off 2,700 employees due to downsizing. And you have to pack your belongings and leave."

She was devastated.

She lost her professional identity.

She also lost her self-worth.

She did not see it coming.

Though she received career counseling, she failed to make any progress in getting a new job. Part of her was reluctant to get a new job because she had a deep fear that she'd be "abandoned" again.

Lucia had a rough childhood. She felt abandoned by her demanding mother. Achieving academic and career success had become her motivation in life. Because it gave her a sense of self-worth. Now, her motivation and self-worth were gone.

With the help of her career advisor, she made it to a few interviews. But she was not hired. She thought her career was over. She stopped trying to get interviews. She thought, "What if I get rejected again? What if…I get the job but can't keep it?"

She was burned out by her own negative thoughts. She had no energy left to pursue opportunities that may lead her to bigger success. She avoided taking actions. She remained lonely and stuck.

REJECTION HURTS

Rejection hurts because it makes you feel less than, not good enough, and helpless. Rejection is different from failure; failure happens to your plans, but rejection happens to you. It is personal. It makes you withdraw. [1] The fear of rejection is crippling because rejection makes you feel shameful (I will talk about self-condemnation and shame in chapter six). You shame yourself. You feel like a humiliation. You stop taking positive actions to get the results you've always wanted. The fear of rejection keeps you from experiencing joy and stepping out of your comfort zone to achieve the success you desire.

Why do we have a fear of rejection?

Rejection means being thrown back. [2] We tend to say, "I was rejected." We use passive voice; this indicates how we feel about the part we play in rejection. Those who have a deep fear of rejection may have been rejected by their caregivers or parents when they were little. If you have felt unloved, unwanted, abandoned, a burden, or simply invisible to your caregivers, then you are more prone to feeling pierced by rejection when you grow up. When we were infants, we were helpless. We had to rely on our caregiver, and our self-worth was tied to our caregivers.

When we get rejected repeatedly, and we know nothing we do seem to prevent us from being rejected; we experience learned helplessness [3]. Psychologists discovered learned helplessness during a series of experiments with dogs. The dogs had previously been shocked repeatedly, and they had "learned" nothing they did would prevent them from the shocks. Eventually, the dogs stopped trying to escape even when they were put in a new environment in which escape was made possible and easy.

Lucia experienced learned helplessness. She was rejected by the company she had devoted her life for over 15 years. However, she couldn't escape the layoff. Though she got interviews, she was not "chosen." She thought there was nothing she could do to escape being rejected. She felt helpless. She stopped trying.

Have you ever been paralyzed by the fear of rejection?

Have you been apprehensive of pursuing big goals for fear of failures and rejection?

If so, this chapter will be beneficial for you.

WHAT'S THE PROBLEM?

When you have the fear of rejection, you will less likely be stepping out of your comfort zone to achieve big goals that matter to you. You may end up missing big opportunities. You may choose not to pursue the success you've dreamed of because you are preoccupied with the fear of rejection. Psychological studies show that our belief in whether we will succeed or fail influences how much effort we'll put into our actions. When you give in to the fear of rejection, your fear may potentially lead you to the onset of depression as well. [4]

What does it mean? That means when you think you will succeed; you are more likely to succeed. When you think you will fail, you will more likely fail. That's a self-fulfilling prophecy. Don't fall into this thinking trap. Because this thinking trap would keep you from achieving the success you've wanted, worst yet, it could even drive you to depression.

Let me give you a few more examples to illustrate the consequences of learned-helplessness.

Let's say; you've been contemplating on a career change. You submitted a dozen resumes and got interviews. But you didn't get any of the jobs that you interviewed for. You thought, "There must be something wrong with my performance. Maybe I am not articulate enough. Maybe I am not smart enough. Maybe…" Rejection hurts. When you were repeatedly rejected, you'd want to quit because it's painful. When you choose to give up prematurely, you won't get what you want.

Let's say you want to start your own business and you need to seek funding from investors. You get rejected many times. When you feel there's nothing you can do to escape from being rejected, you may give up trying. You'll experience learned-helplessness.

Here is another example. Some career advisors say, "Don't ask for the job because it makes you look weak. Let them beg you to take the job." Why would they say so? Because when you don't ask for the job, you won't be rejected directly. It will save you from the pain of rejection. In other words, you hope the hiring manager would offer you the job without you asking for it. But don't ask, don't get. You end up not getting the job.

What's the problem of not asking directly for what you want? Psychologists point out when you make indirect requests; the requests are actually easier to reject. As a result, you are getting more rejections by making indirect requests. That means you make indirect requests because you want to avoid rejections. But you end up getting more rejections! The fear of rejection reduces your chance of success.

Not only that, your fear of rejection could damage your relationships. Here is an example of a couple whose marriage was on the rock. The wife wanted her husband to buy a carton of milk. She was terrified of requesting for fear of rejection. She then made an indirect request. She said, "I know you're really busy. You are always busy with your work. Your career comes first, and I come last. I don't think you would bother helping me. Look, I need to pick up our daughter from school. I just don't have the time to pick up a carton of milk. And there is a load of dirty laundries…" Do you know what happened after the wife made an indirect request with resentment? Her husband rejected her request. He stomped out of the room angrily.

The fear of rejection could potentially ruin your future and damage your relationships. To succeed in life, you need to break the fear of rejection.

HOW TO BREAK THE FEAR OF REJECTION

1. Unlearn Learned Helplessness

When you think there is nothing you can do to resolve a recurring problem, you develop a sense of helplessness. The longer you live with this sense of helplessness, the less likely you are to see options, choices, or what you can do to improve a situation. [5]

But you can unlearn learned helplessness. First of all, you need to know you have options. If you don't see any available options, you can create options. You create options by saying yes to yourself and saying no to many things. You create options by accepting you are not perfect and you don't need to be perfect. You create options by receiving help. You have plenty of options.

You can also train yourself to distinguish irrational worst-case scenario that paralyzes action and the more likely scenarios. This is a thinking skill that enables planning and actions. [6]

Take good care of yourself. Create options for yourself.

2. Grieve for being rejected

You need to grieve for being rejected. Why? Because when you are rejected, you not only lose an opportunity, but you also lose self-love, self-respect, and self-acceptance. Grieving is a psychological process of dealing with a loss. [7] There are five stages of grieving. Initially, the five stages—denial, anger, bargaining, depression, and acceptance—are parts of the process of dealing with the loss of loved ones. However, the framework of grieving is widely used in other settings to help people regain self-trust, self-respect, and self-love.

Let's examine the story of Lucia again. She was emotionally devastated after the layoff because she couldn't handle the rejection. She stayed stuck. After a few months of struggling, she realized she not only lost her job, she also lost a sense of community, security, and self-respect. She felt disoriented, lost, sad, and angry. She became depressed. With the help of her career transition network, she accepted the reality as it was. She got better and happier. However, when she was rejected in job interviews, she regressed to the stage of anger. She lost motivation for fear of rejection. She stopped trying. She needed to go through the grieving cycle all over again to gain back confidence.

The good news—the process of grieving could help us regain our strength after a setback or failure.[8] We can start by noticing our self-criticisms and accept our pain as it is; we will then move toward healing. We can allow ourselves to feel sorrow, loss, fear, loneliness, anger, or whatever feelings arise. As a result, we can all move to a place of self-acceptance.

3. Improve Communication

Research conducted at Stanford University [9] has shown that 9 out of 10 conversations miss the mark. Why? Engaging conversations enable trust and good judgment, thus reducing fears and threats.

Feeling rejected, on the other hand, activates our fear networks, which moves us into protective behaviors.

When was the last time you had a difficult conversation? What happened? Who was involved? What did she/he say that triggered your fear of rejection? How did you react? Or what did you say that triggered the other person's fear of rejection? How did he/she react? What would you like to do differently next time? You may consider "rewriting and retelling" the story in your head. When you change the scripts of your story, you will change your perception of the other person's behaviors. You may also practice self-compassion. That will enable you to employ effective solutions to overcome interpersonal challenges.

4. Gain Acceptance From Supportive Communities

We all experience setbacks in life. It's not a shame of needing other people and getting the support from loving communities. Don't we all need a pat on the shoulder from time to time? Choose your communities, friends, and mentors wisely. Keep a distance from people who are critical, judgmental, and negative. Reject unsolicited advice. Seek wise counsel. Surround yourself with positive, optimistic, like-minded people and communities. I am sure you will bounce back from setbacks faster, and you will overcome the fear of rejection more easily.

*I created the **Train For Joy Private Facebook Community** to connect you with other like-minded people. It is a safe environment where you can give and get a pat on the shoulder. We are all imperfect people, but together, we are more than enough.

ACTIONABLE ADVICE:

- Write in details about your disappointments and setbacks. What happened? What were your reactions?

Now, you are given a chance to rewrite the scripts of your stories. What would your new stories be?

- Write down the names of three positive and trustworthy friends.

- Reach out to your three trusted friends. Tell them your story. Be sure to reject unsolicited advice. You only need a pair of listening ears.

- Write down three things that you appreciate about yourself.

- Write down three things that you want to change. Share with your three trusted friends.

- Write down three accomplishments that you're proud of. Write in details: What happened? Who helped you achieve your goals? How did you feel about yourself? Celebrate your accomplishments.

Claim Your FREE BONUSES:

Download 7 Minutes To Increase Your Happiness FREE Guide (Retail value: $15)

www.gohappyyou.com/p/happiness-hacks

Download 21 Thinking Habits For Success Self-Coaching FREE Workbook (Retail value: $35)

https://www.gohappyyou.com/p/21-thinking-habits-for-success

Get FREE Self-Doubt Detox Strategy Session (Retail value: $375)

https://www.gohappyyou.com/p/self-doubt-detox

Join Train For Joy Private Facebook Community

https://www.facebook.com/groups/256238091871338/?ref=group_header

CHAPTER SIX

SELF-CONDEMNATION

You think, **"That's My Fault."**

Jessica grew up in a dysfunctional family. When she was little, she was regularly accused of making "unforgivable" mistakes. When she's born, her father left the family. She thought she's bad, that's why her father left. She also struggled to gain approvals from her mother.

Her mother had very high expectations of her. Her mother would say, "You ought to win out the boys in school...You ought to be the best..." YOU OUGHT TO, had become an unshakable voice in her subconscious mind.

After graduating from college, she chose to become a teacher. Her mother disapproved of her decision. Under pressure, she resigned and pursued a new career path just to please her mother. She thought that her mother would then be happier. But she was wrong. Her mother continued to have confrontational conversations with her regarding her various decisions about life. This time, as usual, her mother was disappointed and said, "You never listened to me."

Recently, she uncovered a family secret—her mother had a miscarriage before Jessica was conceived. She thought, "If only I had listened to my mother, she would've loved me more. If only I were a good girl, my father wouldn't have left. That's all my fault."

Deep down, she knew nothing she could do would change her mother's opinions of her. Finally, she gave up. She moved a thousand miles away from her mother. But she still couldn't shake off her mother's negative voice on her. She felt guilty, shameful, and condemned.

GUILT, SHAME, AND CONDEMNATION

For those of you who have critical parents, you have accepted a hidden message that you are not good enough or flawed. Also, our society rewards "conventional success"—money, fame, bigger houses, fancy cars, beautiful spouse, and children. You are tempted to beat yourself up for not winning in the game of life. Your inner critic has told you, "You are not good enough. You are not successful enough. You are not beautiful enough." You compare yourself to others. You think to yourself, "My co-workers are more successful than I do. My friend gets a nicer car. My neighbor's yard is more beautiful than mine. My cousin earns more than I do…" Your inner critic relents. Though you hate your inner critic, you deeply believe in her voice. You think there is something wrong with you. You judge yourself. No matter how well you do, you think someone else always seems to be doing better. You sabotage your happiness. You hurt your relationships.

I know self-condemnation firsthand.

The feeling of inferiority had haunted me for many years since childhood. My inner critic condemned, "I should have done better…I should have made better decisions…I should have…" The negative self-talk went on and on.

So, what're the elements of self-condemnation?

This is the definition in the dictionary. Condemnation is to "judge, blame, consider guilty; to proclaim punishment, to state something or somebody is wrong or unacceptable, to force somebody to experience something very unpleasant; to issue an official order that something is unfit to be used; severe reproof, strong censure."

Self-condemnation (or self-judgment) has to do with shame. Shame and guilt are different. **Shame** is the feeling that there is something basically wrong with you. The sense of guilt is about you

DOING something wrong, whereas **shame** is about you BEING wrong at the core. [1]

Self-condemnation involves **self-hatred**. You hate yourself for making mistakes, picking a fight with your spouse, getting a divorce, losing a job, losing the promotion you want, losing your dream house to foreclosure. All in all, you feel not good enough. You feel there is something wrong with you at your core. You seek acceptance and approvals from others. You think you have to pretend to be someone else—someone who is more acceptable and successful to the standard of others. You need to look good on the outside, but you are broken inside.

Has self-condemnation negatively impacted your life?

Let's do a self-check. Be honest with yourself. Take a look at the following statements.

How often do you judge yourself with these statements?

*1. Never; 2. Seldom; 3. Sometimes; 4. Often; 5. Very often

- "I am flawed"

- "I am inadequate"

- "I am not good enough"

- "I am wrong at my core"

- "I am bad"

- "I am unimportant"

- "I am undeserving"

- "I deserve to be miserable"

- "Nothing good would ever happen to me"

- "I deserve ill treatments from others"

- "I am a loser"

- "I am a shame"

- "No one would accept me as I am.

- "I am guilty, ugly, unsuccessful, and bad…"

Self-condemnation could damage your life and your future.

The good news—you can live a better life by developing better thoughts.

HOW WOULD SELF-CONDEMNATION DAMAGE YOUR LIFE?

Self-condemnation can kill your future. It damages your self-image and robs you of your joy. It keeps you from achieving the success you want and reaching your potential. Self-condemnation is also a relationship killer. Your inner critic suggests you're inadequate; then you act like you're deficient.

Ever heard of mirror neurons? Mirror neurons act like mirrors in our brain and reflect others' emotions and behaviors. So, when you mistreat yourself, other people will pick up on that. Don't allow your mirror neurons attract mistreatment. Today, decide to think positively about yourself. You will attract good things when you treat yourself right and think positively about yourself. Because when you treat yourself right, other people will mirror that positive attitude back to you. [2]

You may say, "I know self-condemnation is bad. But I just can't turn off the negative thoughts."

You're right. Sometimes, your self-condemning thoughts seem like broken records playing over and over in your head. But I would like to encourage you. **You are more than your thoughts.** As soon as you notice your negative thoughts, you can write them down and cross them out. You can replace them with positive thoughts. You can take control of your thoughts with deliberate actions. I know it's not easy. I can do it, and I believe you can do that too.

HOW TO BREAK SELF-CONDEMNATION

1. Practice Self-Forgiveness

You are always hard on yourself. You think it's selfish to take care of yourself. You think, "I'm just not good enough, so I need to push myself harder to achieve." You are afraid of making mistakes.

Do you know? You can turn your mistakes into learning opportunities. You are not a loser even if you make mistakes. On the contrary, it is a brave act to learn from your mistakes and decide to do better. You are brave, and you can do that.

Do you know? When you condemn yourself and overcorrect your mistakes, it may lead to fear, anxiety, and depression. A psychologist I met in a professional conference once said, "Forgive the people who hurt you, for they have done the best they could. Forgive yourself, for you have done the best you could."

You have done the best you could, forgive yourself. For the people who judged and damaged you in the past, forgive them. Then you'll begin to live a life that is filled with joy.

2. Practice Self-Compassion

Self-forgiveness and self-compassion are different.

Self-forgiveness is a coping strategy that involves repairing the damage done to your idea of yourself to resolve guilt, shame, disappointment. [3]

Self-compassion goes beyond just forgiving yourself when you've made a mistake. Self-compassion can be applied to any situation of emotional distress. It requires us to recognize our own suffering. [3]

So, how would we recognize our own suffering?

Psychologists suggest we treat ourselves with the same kindness, care, and compassion we would show to a good friend or even a stranger for that matter.

Let me share a personal experience. I believe in Jesus. Jesus said, "Love your neighbors AS yourself." Do I love myself? When I was a young Christian, I didn't love myself. Over the years, I have learned self-love. Now, I tell myself every single day, "Be gentle. Be kind. Be generous to yourself. Jesus is gentle in heart, learn from Him." What do I want to say? You can practice gentleness to yourself, regardless of whether you believe in Jesus or His teaching. But I do.

Also, you need to develop self-awareness. You need to be able to recognize your negative self-talk the moment you hear it. Why? Because when you are aware of your self-judgmental thoughts, you can change them quickly. As soon as you catch your self-judgmental thoughts, you can tell yourself, "I can stop that thought right now. I choose to stop that thought right now." Then, you can replace the negative thought with a positive one. You can also write down the negative thoughts and reflect on them. Ask yourself—how true is that thought?

Ask your loved ones to affirm you. I assume your loved ones are trustworthy, kind, generous, and non-judgmental to you. If they are not, I encourage you to seek professional help. It may be beneficial for you to go through a relationship detox. I have gone through relationship detox in different seasons of my life. To me, it resulted in more clarity, happiness, and fulfillment. I hope you do too. That's freedom!

I WOULD LIKE TO AFFIRM YOU:

- You are creative

- You are talented

- You are resourceful

- You are kind

- You are gentle

- You are generous

- You are successful

- You can create success on your own terms

- You don't need to compare yourself to others

- You are good enough

ACTIONABLE ADVICE:

- Notice your negative self-talk. Write them down as soon as you hear them.

- Cross out your negative thoughts. Replace each one of them with a positive thought.

- Recall what you have done right this week. Recall what your loved ones have done right this week.

- Write down three things that you are grateful for today.

- Quiet yourself. Take 15 minutes to reflect on the situations that are causing you stress. You may feel emotional discomfort. Just relax. Thank yourself. Say this, "Thank you for showing up. Thank you for not giving up. Thank you for everything you have done. You're not alone. Suffering is common to humanity. Now, just be gentle. Listen without judgment." Say to yourself, "I'll be kind to myself. I'll accept myself as I am. I'll forgive myself. I'll be patient with myself."

Claim Your FREE BONUSES:

Download 7 Minutes To Increase Your Happiness FREE Guide (Retail value: $15)

www.gohappyyou.com/p/happiness-hacks

Download 21 Thinking Habits For Success Self-Coaching FREE Workbook (Retail value: $35)

https://www.gohappyyou.com/p/21-thinking-habits-for-success

Get FREE Self-Doubt Detox Strategy Session (Retail value: $375)

https://www.gohappyyou.com/p/self-doubt-detox

Join Train For Joy Private Facebook Community

https://www.facebook.com/groups/256238091871338/?ref=group_header

CLOSING WORDS

Building stronger thinking habits will not only allow you to have more control over your emotional response to stressful situations, but it will also help you monitor your behaviors and build stronger relationships. Eventually, strong thinking habits will promote better well-being and health.

Increasing your happiness and joy isn't about simply reading this book and declaring that you are good enough. Instead, it's about incorporating new thinking strategies into your everyday life so you can remove obstacles and live effectively. Now, your journey of growth and healing has just begun.

Remember, you can build stronger thinking habits by applying the actionable advice of this book. Then, you will begin to keep the toxic beliefs from limiting your life, lessening your self-confidence, and sabotaging your relationships.

Here is a recap of the five toxic beliefs and the solutions.

Your subconscious mind drives your thoughts, feelings, and actions. And your actions will determine the long-term outcomes of your life. Therefore, think right. When you change your thoughts, you can change your life. **Your Action: Think About Your Thoughts; Because You Are More Than Your Thoughts**

You are gentle, kind, and loving. People like you. So people give you responsibilities that you don't ask for. People call you at inconvenient times. You accept any tasks that come your way, and you answer most of the calls. However, you have become exhausted, angry, and stressed. You think, "How come I just can't say no?" Because you feel guilty saying no. **Your Action: Break People-Pleasing; You Can Say NO**

You are in charge of situations, people, and projects. But you never think you are good enough. You think everybody else is doing better than you do. You believe that you are inadequate and mediocre although evidence shows you are highly skilled and you are the expert. Paradoxically, you may even have a fear of success. **Your Action: Say NO To Self-Doubting; You Are Good Enough**

You set an exceptionally high standard for yourself and/or others. You believe you need to be perfect, and you expect the people around you to be perfect. You are resentful when you or others do not meet your high standard. You become depressed when not achieving your goals. It's a painful journey living as a perfectionist. **Your Action: Say NO To Perfectionism; Because No One Is Perfect**

Rejection hurts. Because it makes you feel less than, not enough, and helpless. Rejection is different from failure; failure happens to your plans, but rejection happens to you. The good news is that you can unlearn helplessness and overcome the fear of rejection. You can create options for yourself. You can also gain self-acceptance through deliberate actions. **Your Action: Say NO To The Fear of Rejection; You Can Take Risks**

You have a negative inner critic, and you judge yourself all the time. You tell yourself, "I should have been more successful," "I should have done better," "I should have been a better spouse and parent," "I should have been perfect," "I should have landed that job or earned that promotion." You compare yourself with others and feel falling short. **Your Action: Stop Condemning Yourself; Because That's Not Your Fault**

You are more than your thoughts. You can change your thoughts. You can unlearn helplessness and learn to be optimistic. You have more control over the outcomes of your life than you think. When you change your thoughts, you can change your life. Let's train for joy. **Your Action: You Are Made For More; You Can Train Yourself For Joy**

WORDS OF ENCOURAGEMENT

Even though we have little control over our circumstances, we have complete control over our reactions, attitudes, and explanations of any stressful life events. You are more than your thoughts. You can overcome any adversities. Your beliefs determine whether you will achieve your big dreams and goals. You can accomplish any goals you set your mind to. You can obtain any success you want. You can reshape your life and rewrite your memories by changing your thoughts and the explanations of your adversity.

FINAL THOUGHTS

I now believe we are not to brag about the plans we have for tomorrow, for we don't have a clue what tomorrow may bring to us.

However,

When life gives you lemons, you can train yourself for joy.

When life throws you a curveball, you can choose to bounce forward.

You are made for more...

I hope you'll hold on to good thoughts and sound beliefs, and you'll be courageous when facing failures. I hope you'll have the wisdom to know what you can change and have the courage to turn any adversities into victories. You'll bounce forward and thrive. You'll live a good life.

When you think about your thoughts...

You know you are more than your thoughts.

When you change your thoughts...

You will change your life, and you will live a good life.

You have already known...

You can achieve your big dreams, and

You can create the success of your own terms

Because…

You are made for more.

And you are trained for joy.

Claim Your FREE BONUSES:

Download 7 Minutes To Increase Your Happiness FREE Guide (Retail value: $15)

www.gohappyyou.com/p/happiness-hacks

Download 21 Thinking Habits For Success Self-Coaching FREE Workbook (Retail value: $35)

https://www.gohappyyou.com/p/21-thinking-habits-for-success

Get FREE Self-Doubt Detox Strategy Session (Retail value: $375)

https://www.gohappyyou.com/p/self-doubt-detox

Join Train For Joy Private Facebook Community

https://www.facebook.com/groups/256238091871338/?ref=group_header

COACHING PROGRAMS For Your Success And Happiness:

https://www.gohappyyou.com/p/programs

TrainForJoy™ -Learned Positively! Group Coaching

TransformU™—From Fears To Actions! Webinar Coaching

TheGoalGym™ Achieve Anything You Want! Individual Coaching

MobileU™—Combat The Daily Grind! Text-Based Coaching

Your Joy Coach & Success Strategist, Corinna Kong

Increase Your Happiness. Achieve Your Dreams. GO! Happy You!

www.gohappyyou.com

Connect with me on social media

Facebook: @trainforjoy @gohappyyou

Instagram: @corinna.kong

Pinterest: https://www.pinterest.com/corinnakong/

LinkedIn: https://www.linkedin.com/in/corinnakong

Please leave a book review on Amazon. Your reviews are important. Thank you!

ABOUT THE AUTHOR

Corinna Kong, M.Ed. has a background in medical social work, educational technology, and leadership and organization development. She empowered over 2,700 families to overcome insurmountable challenges in her first career as a medical social worker. For the past 14 years, she has helped Fortune 500 technology companies, startups, and NGOs in Silicon Valley design professional and leadership development roadmaps that enabled over 7,000 professionals and leaders to achieve their success.

She empowers achievers like you to increase your happiness and achieve your dreams. She leverages her knowledge of NeuroLeadership Results Coaching System™, the new psychology of success, and her experience building a happy workplace to reveal a happy you.

For the past few years, she has endeavored to enable young children in underprivileged communities to learn better and gain more confidence. Her favorite nonprofit organizations are All Students Matters, Ravenswood Educational Foundation, and Reading Partners. Her dream is to help the young children achieve academic and life goals and become leaders in their communities.

Other than that, she has also served as an Associate Director in the Silicon Valley Healing Rooms where she imparted hope and joy to people under insurmountable circumstances.

She was born in Hong Kong and has resided in Silicon Valley, California since 1998.

INTRODUCTION

1. Retrieved July 8, 2018, from http://www.tecweb.org/styles/gardner.html

CHAPTER ONE: THINK ABOUT YOUR THOUGHTS

1. Eric R. Kandel, *In Search of Memory: The Emergence of a New Science of Mind* (NY: Norton, 2006).
2. Leaf, Caroline, *Switch On Your Brain: The Key to Peak Happiness, Thinking, and Health* (MI: Baker Books, 2013)
3. Retrieved June 10, 2018, from https://www.inc.com/geoffrey-james/use-neuroscience-to-make-you-successful.html
4. Retrieved June 10, 2018, from http://www.apa.org/monitor/2015/02/bad-memories.aspx
5. Seligman, E. P. Martin, *Learned Optimism: How to Change Your Mind and Your Life* (NY: Vintage Books, 2006)
6. Seligman, E. P. Martin, Flourish: *A Visionary New Understanding of Happiness and Well-being* (NY: Free Press, 2012)

CHAPTER TWO: PEOPLE-PLEASING

1. Ware, Bronnie, *The Top Five Regrets of the Dying: A Life Transformed by the Dearly Departing* (US: Hay House, 2012)
2. Retrieved February 22, 2018, from Success Magazine

CHAPTER THREE: SELF-DOUBTING

1. Retrieved March 3, 2018, from https://www.psychologytoday.com/us/blog/minority-report/201406/asian-shame-and-honor
2. Retrieved February 11, 2018, from http://reset.me/story/neuroplasticity-the-10-fundamentals-of-rewiring-your-brain/
3. Retrieved February 11, 2018, from https://twitter.com/drcynthiamd?lang=en
4. Retrieved February 18, 2018, from https://www.thebestbrainpossible.com
5. Retrieved February 18, 2018, from https://www.inc.com/geoffrey-james/use-neuroscience-to-make-you-successful.html

6. Retrieved February 11, 2018, from
   https://www.entrepreneur.com/article/242373

CHAPTER FOUR: PERFECTIONISM

1. Retrieved March 5, 2018, from
   http://www.drmargaretjordan.com/perfectionism/
2. Retrieved March 5, 2018, from
   https://www.psychologytoday.com/us/articles/199905/the-perfect-trap

CHAPTER FIVE: FEAR OF REJECTION

1. Ortberg, John, *I'd Like You More If You Were More like Me: Getting Real about Getting Close* (US: Tyndale Online, 2017)
2. Retrieved March 5, 2018, from
   https://www.psychologytoday.com/us/blog/talking-apes/201607/ask-and-you-shall-receive
3. Retrieved March 5, 2018, from
   https://www.psychologytoday.com/us/blog/thriving101/201012/rejection-losers-guide
4. Psychology Today
5. Retrieved March 7, 2018, from
   http://www.rogerkallen.com/unlearning-helplessness/
6. Southwick, Steven & Cherney, Dennis, *Resilience: The Science of Mastering Life's Greatest Challenges* (NY: Cambridge University Press, 2018)
7. Retrieved March 15, 2018, from
   https://www.biography.com/people/elisabeth-kubler-ross-262762
8. Retrieved March 15, 2018, from
   https://www.psychologytoday.com/us/experts/john-amodeo-phd-mft
9. Retrieved March 15, 2018, from http://levelupleadership.com/9-out-of-10-conversations-miss-the-mark/

CHAPTER SIX: SELF-CONDEMNATION

1. Retrieved March 20, 2018, from
   https://www.huffingtonpost.com/margaret-paul-phd/dealing-with-shame_b_994991.html

2. Leaf, Caroline, *Switch On Your Brain: The Key to Peak Happiness, Thinking, and Health* (MI: Baker Books, 2013)
3. Retrieved March 25, 2018, from
   http://www.apa.org/pubs/journals/cou/index.aspx

JOURNAL AND NOTES